ROB GUTRO

KINDRED
SPIRITS

WHEN A MEDIUM BEFRIENDS A SPIRIT

To Michelle
Always be
a good spirit!
Rob G

Cover Photo

The cover shows two men who have become kindred spirits, one in the physical world and one in the afterlife. It was created by Got You Covered @CoversByLisa. www.facebook.com/CoversByLisa.

Dedication

This book is dedicated to the memory of Ed G., who passed in December, 1996. Ed showed me that being a medium means that you can also befriend someone you never met in the physical world and learn so much about them that you consider them a close friend.

Contents

Foreword

Introduction

Chapter 1: My Super-power
Chapter 2: How is Befriending a Spirit Possible?
Chapter 3: Dead Men (and Others) Talking
Chapter 4: How Did Ed's Spirit Befriend Me?
Chapter 5: Meeting Ed's Spirit
Chapter 6: Getting to Know Ed
Chapter 7: Lunch Date with a Spirit
Chapter 8: Ed's Spirit Treasure Hunt: How Mediumship Works
Chapter 9: Ed Finally Adopts a Dog
Chapter 10: Ed's Birthday Wishes
Chapter 11: Ed Adopts Buzz
Chapter 12: Stop the Clock!
Chapter 13: Spirits Can Go Anywhere
Chapter 14: Amazing Rescue in England
Chapter 15: Sign of the M.O.T.
Chapter 16: A Push from my "Ghost Writer"
Chapter 17: Rescued in the Street
Chapter 18: Ed's Lessons to All

Bibliography

About the Author

Introduction

I wrote this book to show how amazing people in spirit can be, even long after their physical bodies are gone. By reading about Ed's interactions with me you'll find that the types of messages can apply to the 8 billion people on planet Earth.

I've learned a lot about this life and the next from my inherited ability to sense ghosts and spirits. I have learned the difference between a ghost and a spirit, and this book will touch on them. However, the main purpose of this short book is to show you how it is possible to get to know someone in spirit even to the point where you feel as if you've made a close friend. Children have been known to say this about earthbound ghosts that they see.

This book compiles the many messages I have received from a very special spirit over the last 14 years to show you spirits are still around us. His name is Ed, and he is someone passed away before I got to meet him in the physical world.

As you read through the interactions I have had with Ed's spirit, you'll learn about many of the ways your own loved ones in spirit are trying to communicate with you. So, although this book may tell my story, it tells the stories of billions of people who lost someone.

Ed showed me that being a medium means that you can also befriend someone you never met in the physical world by learning so much about them that you consider them a close friend.

In the 'Spirit Treasure Hunt' chapter, Ed took me on an incredible journey that provided so many personal and unique signs that I was able to bring his dad peace after 15 long years of grieving.

I hope that this book provides insight and a better understanding that the spirits of our loved ones are around us from time to time, and guide and help us.

This book concludes with several lessons for everyone, as a result of Ed's interactions from the other side

Hopefully by reading this, you will open yourself up to receiving or seeing messages that you may have overlooked before. You just need to be aware of it.

###

Chapter 1
My Super-power

Hello! My name is Rob. I consider myself a typical, middle-aged guy who happens to be a scientist (meteorologist), has a spouse, four dogs and lives in the suburbs.

My Italian mother made sure I could get by in the kitchen, sew and nurse people and pets back to health, for which I am eternally grateful. I've been working with dog rescues and doing fundraising for them for over a decade. I enjoy meeting new people and animals, and that includes those in spirit. As a typical guy, I love books that include mysteries, current affairs, science and superheroes and comic books.

Mediums can sense the energy from people or animals who have passed on. I consider it a "super-power." Mediums can sometimes see physical forms or see them in their mind. They can hear and feel those who have passed on and sense their emotions. I can do those things, but usually see them in my mind (and sketch them out like a comic book).

So, how did this super-power come about? When I was a teenager, I realized I had the ability to see, sense and communicate with earthbound ghosts and spirits. I learned it runs on my mother's side of the family. That whole story is in my *Ghosts and Spirits* book. I'm a medium, although I've jokingly called myself a "medium rare" (because I'm always learning).

This gift doesn't define who I am; it's just a part of me, as it is of so many others I've met since I wrote my first book, "*Ghosts and Spirits: Insights from a Medium.*" I've written several books about my experiences with people and pets who have passed away. In fact, I receive so many messages from pets I've developed a reputation of being a "pet medium" although I communicate with everyone on the other side.

For decades I didn't pay much attention to my abilities, because I didn't understand them and I wasn't spiritually or emotionally mature enough to do so. In 2005 my puppy Buzz passed and re-opened the door to the other side for me. It was Buzz's many communications that inspired me to start writing books to convey to others how spirits and ghosts communicate, to bring them understanding and comfort.

Later, when I fell in love, my abilities increased a hundred-fold. Since my abilities re-awakened, I always get a dull headache in the presence of a ghost or spirit (and there is a difference).

Because I'm a scientist, I believe in the science of energy. Energy is the foundation of the afterlife. Both earth-bound ghosts and spirits whom have crossed over (like Ed), draw on physical and emotional energies. They use that energy to get strong enough to send a sign that they are around. As you read through the book, you'll identify different types of signs.

Being a medium means sometimes learning how to put together puzzle pieces of information from those who passed. Sometimes mediums get direct messages. Other times they get random words, pictures, names, dates and thoughts and they are usually very personal to the entity communicating with them. The trick is figuring out the message.

After developing those abilities, I still didn't realize I could actually get to know a spirit as I know and befriend living people. But that's what happened. I've become familiar with Ed through words, personality and heart. It was like getting to know him over many years.

I am not a medium who charges a fee for readings because I am still developing my "super-power." I do try to help grieving people whenever I can. Like Clark Kent, I have a career (not at a large metropolitan newspaper), to put a roof over my head and take care of my family. I use my gifts like a hobby to help bring comfort to people who need to understand their loved ones are still very much around them.

###

Chapter 2
How is Befriending a Spirit Possible?

Since the success of the *Long Island Medium* television program, people have been going to mediums more than ever before.

If you've ever watched an episode of *Long Island Medium* or been to a live show hosted by a medium, you know that mediums will receive only snippets of information.

Often, after the message has been received and related to the intended recipient, the medium tends to forget what the spirit told us. That's because we channel the spirit and are just repeating what they are telling us. Often, we're not really able to remember entirely what they say. That's why mediums tell people to bring recorders or write things down during readings.

So, it's really not too common that a medium gets to continually know a spirit, one who crossed into the light, because they don't come around the medium often and over a long period of time. That means that a medium can't really get to know a spirit like they know a living person whom they perhaps meet for lunch each month or talk with on the phone. That is, unless that spirit keeps coming back over and over and sharing personal information just as a friend does.

That's what happened in the case of the spirit this book is about. His name is Ed, and he's been coming around me for almost 15 years, and I expect he'll be around until I join him on the other side.

So, how does getting snippets of information from Ed's spirit over the last 15 years make me feel close enough to him to consider him a "kindred spirit"? It's because I now have great insight into his thoughts, his sense of humor, his quirkiness and his love of family and friends.

Every time Ed has provided me a message from his memories in the physical it was like I heard a friend telling me about himself, and sharing things that he wouldn't share with just anyone.

Ed also clued me into the fact that he is the one who likely introduced me to his former partner. That's something that a spirit does - brings people together that need to meet.

As you read about the experiences Ed has shared, you'll see that he's also been there to rescue me in other ways, including when my husband, Tom, and I were lost in England.

He's also been the friend I needed when one of our dogs passed away. Ed gave me that assurance and physical proof that he was there to welcome our dog Sprite to the afterlife.

In short, Ed's spirit has confided things to me, he's been there when I needed him, and he's come whenever I've called him. We also share things in common, including close birthdays. Those are the many reasons why I consider Ed a "Kindred Spirit."

###

Chapter 3
Dead Men (and Others) Talking

This is how my communicating with those who passed began. I was just 13 years old when my grandfather, Giramondo, appeared to me as a full body apparition. He looked exactly as he appeared in life; dressed in slacks, wearing a button down shirt, suspenders, and eyeglasses. Even though he died at the age of 76, his hair was still mostly black with just a few streaks of gray, and he had a pencil thin moustache.

At the time of my grandfather's visit, I was home alone with our family's dog, Gigi, a small 10-pound white poodle. My mother often referred to Gigi as "her favorite child," something she was fond of saying especially in the presence of my two brothers and I.

From the kitchen where I was sitting, I had a clear vantage point through the dining room into the living room. Odd lights from all corners of the living room began to coalesce in the middle of the room. As I continued to stare at the small orbs of light coming together, they formed the shape of a person. In what seemed like minutes, but was likely only seconds, there stood my grandfather in full color.

Because it was my first time seeing a spirit, I panicked. I grabbed Gigi and ran out of the house. I sat on the steps outside and waited for my parents to return. After telling them of my experience, it was then that my mother revealed that she also had the "gift," but was too afraid to use it.

It was July 1977. That was significant because it was the month of his birthday. Since then I've learned that spirits often "visit" around the time of birthdays, anniversaries, and holidays. An important point to remember, because it certainly applies to Ed's re-appearances.

As I grew older, I ignored my abilities. I was caught up in my life, going to school, working multiple jobs, moving several times, starting a career, all in an effort to find my place in the world. That was a lot of distraction, and distraction creates white noise in your head if you're sensitive to spirit, and this white noise inadvertently blocks out the ghosts and spirits... with some exceptions.

It wasn't until I was in an established career and a stable home, that I finally felt settled. That's when I was able to once again tune in and focus on signs from spirit. Unfortunately, it took a tragic event to jumpstart my abilities.

In 2005, my puppy, Buzz, was tragically killed. He was such an amazing communicator that it was as if he had turned on a firehose from the afterlife. Buzz reawakened my gift and in doing so, brought peace and comfort by reminding me that he was still very much around.

Soul 101 and a Spirit versus a Ghost

Before I continue, I need to give a lesson in what I call "Soul 101." That is, what happens after every living thing's physical body dies? What I have learned from talking with spirit is that the energy that courses through our bodies combines with our memories, personalities, and knowledge gained while we were alive. That forms a "soul." Everything living thing has one - people and animals.

I also need to explain the difference between a spirit and a ghost. A spirit is an entity who has crossed over into the Light (and joins the energies that run through the cosmos) and a ghost is an entity who chooses to remain earthbound, usually in a fixed location and motivated by a specific reason.

Spirits can come back to visit loved ones wherever and whenever they have a message they want to communicate. In fact, they can appear anywhere on Earth and even at multiple places at the same time. It goes beyond our understanding and limitations of physics. Unlike spirits, ghosts are fixed in a specific place where they have chosen to spend their eternity.

How Does a Medium Get Messages?

So what does a medium actually get from people or pets in the afterlife? Well, to start, mediums read energy. Just like when you walk into a room full of living people and you're drawn to some of them. Conversely, you may feel as if you want to avoid others. You're reading their energy and it either jives with yours or doesn't. In a similar vein, mediums read energy, too, but the energies of people or animals who have passed.

As a medium, I can hear them, feel them, see them in my mind, and on a rare occasion I can see them in physical form (but it takes a lot of energy for them to actually make that happen). They share words, pictures, dates, songs, places, names, events, books, movies, and more.

I use my abilities as a medium with a paranormal investigation team called "Inspired Ghost Tracking of Maryland, also known as IGT. The group investigate unusual activities in private homes and historic places. Private residences are of prime importance to the group because intelligent haunts or interactive ghosts who house themselves in a home can cause a lot of problems, despite the ghost's personality.

IGT helps cross ghosts into the light and out of the earthbound location, so the ghost can find peace with their family members on the other side. It also helps the people currently living in the home and stops the usually unnerving paranormal activity, so it's a win-win situation. You can read about many IGT cases in my other books.

Whenever I go on paranormal investigations (of earthbound ghosts) I usually bring a notebook and sketch out what a ghost looks like. So far, every ghost I've drawn has been identified as being the one haunting the location I was investigating.

Both ghosts and spirits also share their pain of death with me and other mediums- that is, the physical feelings they endured before they died. They convey those things to prove their identity. As such, throughout all of the paranormal investigations I've been on, and places I've visited, I've been hit, punched, pushed down stairs, felt as if I were stabbed, shot, bludgeoned, sliced with a sword, hit by bricks, and felt heart attacks, cancer, kidney failure, etc. from ghosts and spirits.

Making Sense of the Puzzle Pieces

What's important here, is that the things ghosts or spirits tell mediums usually come in fragments or pieces. It's not like talking to someone on the phone. Mediums will hear the most important word or word and not an entire sentence sometimes. We may head a date, and not the meaning of it, so we have decipher its meaning.

Being a medium is like sitting in front of a 1,000 piece puzzle of messages from the dead, and trying to put them together in a cohesive way that it paints a clear and full picture of what the ghost or spirit is trying to communicate.

I didn't ask for this gift to communicate with people and pets who have passed, but over time I have embraced it and used it to help comfort others. Most times, it's up to the person for whom the messages are intended to make sense out of the puzzle pieces.

What this Book Means to Readers

By reading this book, you will understand different ways that a spirit can communicate with you. Ed's methods of communications were not solely limited to messages I received telepathically as a medium. Ed provided physical signs, he moved things, led me to objects and led people to me on purpose so that I would know he is around.

Any spirit who has crossed over into the light can do those things. Ghosts, however, can only do them in the fixed location of their choosing. Spirits can do things anywhere and they can also influence living things in nature to act erratically to give a hint of their presence.

So, as a reader, this amazing story of how Ed befriended me as a medium is not limited to me. It can happen to you, too, if you're sensitive or open to it.

###

Chapter 4
How Did Ed's Spirit Befriend Me?

Now that you know spirits and ghosts give snippets of messages, or puzzle pieces, you're likely wondering how I could possibly feel as if I've really befriended a spirit.

Ed isn't just a spirit that comes around from time to time as spirits of loved ones generally do. As I mentioned in the previous chapter, spirits appear usually on special occasions and then disappear for a while. That's not Ed, however. Ed is around me a lot! In fact, when I met Tom I told him, "there are three people in this relationship, and it appears that's the way it's always going to be. Ed's spirit is around often." What's funny, is that sometimes Tom feels like it's "two against one!"

As you'll read in the following chapters, Ed has been around me for a decade and a half, continually giving me information about himself and those who knew him during his time in the physical world.

Ed has revealed his personality to me, especially his fun side. He's shown me that he loves and cares for his family. He's provided insight into his life on Earth and things he said and did that only people who befriended him during his time here would know. Whenever I would voice those things, people who knew him were and are astounded (as am I)!

A photo of Ed is included in the montage hanging on the wall going up the stairs to the second floor of our house. Each night, as I walk down stairs, I say good night to Ed, as well as to the photos of my parents, and our dogs Buzz and Sprite, all of whom are in spirit. I talk with them all each night (and yes, sometimes they talk back!) However, Ed talks to me the most and he's not just a person in spirit. He's a "Kindred Spirit" and a close friend.

In the next chapter, you'll read about the closeness of my birthdate with Ed's and how other things appear to be coincidences. The one thing I tell everyone is that "When it comes to spirits, there are no coincidences." Spirits make things happen for a reason.

###

Chapter 5
Meeting Ed's Spirit

Ed G. and I never met in the physical world. In fact, I never knew who he was until almost 20 years after he had passed away.

I didn't learn about Ed through his family or his friends. The person that told me about Ed was Tom, the guy I would marry in 2009. When I met Tom, I asked about previous relationships. Tom mentioned he and Ed were partners in the 1990s.

Tom didn't like to talk about his past, so getting any information about Ed was a challenge, so I didn't press him. I only knew of Ed's name and that he worked in landscaping. Tom and Ed were together almost 9 years before deciding to go their separate ways.

Spirits Make Things Happen for a Reason

As I mentioned, birthdays and other special dates are key times when spirits give us messages or guide us. As I'm writing this book, Ed's spirit opened my eyes about the timing of events. I know now that it was Ed's spirit that arranged for Tom to find my online profile in November 2005. I realize that Ed had a hand in our meeting, because Tom found me on the week of Tom's birthday. Ed was around Tom during the week of his birthday and introduced us as a "birthday present."

Spirits do that. They influence us to do things. They nudge us to drive a different way home from work and we later learn that an accident had occurred on our normal route. They protect us. They guide us to do things to better our lives because they want the best for us.

I've learned that I have several things in common with Ed. Although born two years apart, the date of our birth is 2 days apart. Ed and I are both communicators and we are both optimistic. Another thing I found interesting was that Ed loved reading one particular comic book, "Uncle Scrooge." Tom later told me that Ed would read those comics and howl with laughter. I also read comics, but I love the superhero variety.

The Mystery and Tragedy of Ed's Passing

After I met Tom and learned that Ed was his ex-partner, I inquired as to where Ed was today. Tom told me that he had passed away sometime in the early morning hours of December 19, 1996 in Virginia, at age 35. At the time of his death, Ed was staying with a relative, and was found unresponsive in his bedroom, when the relative attempted to awaken him. An autopsy was performed and the cause of death was determined to be suicide. That conclusion haunted Ed's father for many years until our visit in 2011, when the true cause of his passing was revealed.

In that year, Ed's spirit took us on a "spirit treasure hunt" that altered the perceived end of his life and brought relief to his dad. You'll read about that grand adventure in a later chapter. The story also appeared in my book *Lessons Learned from Talking to the Dead.*

In the next chapter, you'll read about how Ed's spirit revealed himself to me for the first time, and gave me what would be the beginning of many messages. It would be the beginning of a special friendship with a spirit.

###

Chapter 6
Getting to Know Ed

This chapter originally appeared in my book "Ghosts and Spirits: Insights from a Medium."

Whenever I speak of Ed, I tell others that he's like a friend who lives in another state. That's one way to look at someone you lost, as if they are living in another place, because they can and do come back to give you messages and help you make decisions.

Through Ed's communications in spirit, I've learned about his personality, his quick wit, and dry sense of humor. He's shared some of his memories, some of his favorite possessions, his likes and dislikes, connections with his family and even a nickname he called someone.

In this chapter, you'll read about some signs, symbols and memories that Ed's spirit shared with me to prove that he's still around.

Why Does Ed's Spirit Keeping Coming To Me?

Spirits know who can hear them and see them. Ed knew I had this ability, so he kept the lines of communications open. After all, he had a lot to talk about. Just like people are talkative in the physical world, they don't lose that characteristic in the afterlife.

Spirits and even earthbound ghosts know that they can go to certain people who have the gift of mediumship, in order to be heard. While Earth bound ghosts usually want to be heard to get help crossing over, spirits (who have crossed) want us to know they're with us and they love us. They're not usually asking for anything, other than having a medium tell the spirit's living relatives that they are still very much around. In Ed's case, though, he wanted to share memories of his past, and give me inside information about Tom.

First Contact: A Physical Appearance

The first time I sensed Ed's spirit was in the summer of 2007. Tom and I had been on a quick day trip to Virginia to visit the cemetery where many of Tom's ancestors are buried, so I was already tuned in to spirit. We were on our way back home when Ed came in.

I had seen several photographs of Ed, so I knew what he looked like. He was handsome, stood about 5 feet 10 inches tall, with a slender build, dark hair, and a nice smile.

(Photo: Ed. Credit: T.W)

As the drive continued, I got the urge to look in the rearview mirror. When I did, I was looking at his smiling face looking back at me. It was startling.

I told Tom that Ed was in the back seat. Tom wasn't surprised, because he's felt Ed around him. What was surprising though, was that I told him I actually saw Ed's face looking into my rearview mirror.

That was the first time I realized that Ed was letting us know he is absolutely around us and he'd be "in it for the long haul."

Ed's Presence Confirmed by Another

Several months later, in September 2007, we received confirmation from another source that Ed was around us when we visited a pair of psychic mediums, a mother-daughter team, in Ellicott City, Maryland.

A psychic can tune into the energy of the past, present and future, and a medium can communicate with the past. These women had both of those gifts. I am just a medium and don't have the psychic gift.

We had been to see them once before. But on this occasion, we were separated into different rooms. Each of them gave us the same message: Tom and I are other's soul mate.

This time the psychic that met with Tom told him some very interesting things that involved Ed. She asked him if he had a previous partner that had passed. He said "yes." The psychic then told him that his late partner was still around and watching over him. She related that Ed was telling her that "Tom had found his soul mate in Rob."

The psychic then said we would move in together before the end of the year. At that time, Tom told her he didn't believe that would happen (recalling our conversation in the summer that he wasn't ready).

Ed Influences a Big Decision

Two months passed. During that time, we had finished most of the renovations on my townhouse (we eventually wanted to sell it, but were under no timetable). One day after work, Tom drove up to my townhouse for dinner and came inside exasperated from the traffic and said "We need to consolidate." It was the week before Thanksgiving, and just as the psychic indicated in September, it was before the end of the year. Had Ed's spirit influenced all of this? I don't know for sure, but I have a strong feeling he did because he was the one feeding the psychic information from the other side.

A Nickname Revealed on an Anniversary

Spirits are known for giving signs of their presence or messages for loved ones on birthdays or anniversaries, and that includes anniversaries of their passing as well. Ed's spirit came through on the week that marked the twelfth anniversary of his passing.

During the weekend before Christmas in 2008, Tom and I were out shopping. I wasn't particularly thinking of Ed or anything else other than shopping. What I didn't realize is that the anniversary date of Ed's passing was the very next week, a prime time for a spirit to say hello.

I suddenly heard in my head "Call him "M.O.T." So I said aloud, "You M.O.T." I asked Tom if this had any meaning to him.

Tom stopped in his tracks and asked, "Who told you to call me that?" I responded, "Edward." Ed wasn't physically walking beside us, but he was there in spirit and he told me to say that.

I wondered why Tom looked so shocked. He said that Ed always called him a "Mean Old Thing." It gave me insight into Ed's playful personality. So Ed was letting us know that he's still around 12 years after the date of his passing.

Ed would again use that same acronym in 2012 when we were on vacation in England, an adventure you'll read about later in this book.

How Spirit Influences Things

Spirits can influence us to say things we wouldn't normally say, look in places we would not normally look, go somewhere we wouldn't usually go, or do something we would never think to do, all to give us a hint that they are around us. When this happens, we truly know that there is no such thing as a coincidence when it comes to spirit.

That same kind of spirit suggestion occurred in January, 2009. One night Tom mentioned that he would like to sense Ed. He knew that I had been receiving messages from Ed since 2005 (when I met Tom), but he wanted to get a sign from Ed without Ed telling me something. I told Tom to simply ask for a sign.

Spirits can hear us, and they want to comfort us, so all you have to do is ask. In fact, you can either speak your wish aloud or think it, because both sound and thoughts are energy. Sometimes, though, it takes a while to come through to us because it requires them to obtain enough energy to make something happen.

To learn more about the different types of energy spirits and ghosts draw on, you can read more about the importance of energy in my *Ghosts and Spirits* and *Lessons Learned from Talking to the Dead* books.

###

Chapter 7
Lunch Date with a Spirit

You never know when a spirit is going to drop in. Usually though, when several people get together and talk about them they're bound to make an appearance. That's exactly what happened when Tom and I met Ed's friend, Robert, in January, 2010 for lunch. I will say that the benefit of also meeting a spirit for lunch is that they don't run up a tab.

That lunch date was the first time that Robert and Tom were physically in the same room since Ed's memorial services 13 years before.

Because I never knew Ed when he was alive in the physical world, I didn't know his friends, either. So, meeting an old friend of Ed's was like meeting another piece of Ed's heart and provided a little further insight into his personality.

We usually befriend people that we have things in common with, or that we feel good around. I could see how Ed's and Robert's personalities were similar mostly because they seem to have the same dry sense of humor.

Although I had known about Ed since December 2005, it wasn't until this meeting over four years later, that I would encounter Robert. That's because Robert lives in central Virginia, which several hours away. Robert happened to come into the Washington, D.C. area for an event and contacted us.

Before Ed passed, he lived with Robert for a short time in central Virginia. Over lunch, Robert relayed several stories of Ed's spirit visiting him in his house since his passing.

A Sign in Ed's Dishwasher Habit

Robert told us when Ed was his roommate in the mid-1980s, Ed had a habit of always running the dishwasher. Robert told us that after Ed passed away, Robert would walk into the kitchen and noticed the dishwasher had turned itself on.

Robert said that he knew that it was Ed who had been the one to start it.

Spirits Love Electrical Things

Spirits will often play with electrical things because it's easy for them to do. After all, spirits are energy. That's why sometimes lights flicker when a ghost or spirit is around. As energy, they have the ability to manipulate it, drain it to manifest, or use it to make noises among other things.

When my dad passed in 2008, he started playing with the light in my mother's hallway. That light had never malfunctioned over the 50 years they were in that house. My mother even had it checked by 2 electricians after my dad passed and there was nothing wrong with it. She finally acknowledged it was my dad playing with the light to let her know she wasn't alone.

Sometimes whenever I called my mom and she was walking through the hallway, I could tell when dad's spirit was flickering the light because I would hear my mother tell him to "cut it out!"

Ed's Spirit Walks In

Getting back to lunch with Robert. While Tom and Robert were talking, I sensed Ed's spirit enter.

I always know when a spirit or ghost walks into a room because I develop a dull headache in the back left side of my head. Since they are energy, I liken the headache's cause to an energy overload in my brain, triggering the ache. Although I don't know why it occurs in that part of my head, I have heard other mediums and sensitive people describe the same sensation in the same place. Maybe that's where the "supernatural receptors" are located.

The headache showed up and suddenly Ed's spirit filled me with feelings of his love and friendship for Tom and Robert. Although I couldn't see him, I sensed him sitting in the chair next to Robert.

Telepathically, Ed told me to say aloud to Tom and Robert, "I screwed up." So I said it. They stopped and looked at me, thinking it was me talking. I told them those were Ed's exact words, and that he was sitting at the table with us.

Ed had me tell them he did something that led to his passing. In the next year, he would reveal to me how he "screwed up" and solve the mystery of exactly how his life ended. You'll read about that in the next chapter.

Ed asked me to repeat after him. So I did. I told Robert and Tom that Ed says, "Stop talking about the funeral and talk about the funny things they used to do together."

As we were served lunch, I heard Ed say, "Tell them I love 'em," in his rich Virginia twang, something I learned he held onto even in the afterlife.

As Tom and Robert continued to talk, I'm sure I appeared distracted because I was trying to also listen to Ed.
Despite Ed's plea to not discuss the end of his life, Tom and Robert persisted rehashing memories from Ed's memorial service.

That was enough for Ed to toss out something totally random to get them to think about something else; something they hadn't thought about in decades.

Ed said to me, "Ask them about a silver car." Of course, I had no idea what kinds of cars he owned.

Ed projected a picture in my mind of a small car. Anyone who knows me, knows that I couldn't tell one car from another, and I always joke that's why I drive a pick-up truck.

I interrupted Tom and Robert and said "Ed wanted me to bring up his car." I said, "Ed says it was a small, silver colored car, and that you'll remember it."

For a moment, Tom and Robert tried to picture the car. At first they noted that Ed owned a small landscaping business and that he couldn't possibly have had a small car. But then the memory seemed to hit them at the same time and they both laughed.

They remembered that Ed did indeed own a small car, a 1983 Toyota Corolla, silver in color. They laughed because they said he use to load all of his landscaping tools into the back seat, even a lawnmower, and would roll down the back windows, and drive down the road with the handles from all of the tools protruding out of the open windows.

That reference to a silver car was Ed's way of proving that he was sitting with his friends at lunch once again.

What Spirits Want for Us

Most importantly, Ed brought up the funny memory of the silver car to get Tom and Robert to stop dwelling on the end of Ed's life and focus on something positive. Spirits want us to remember good things, fun things. They don't want us to continually recall their death of funeral.

They want us to talk about the things they did in the physical world that made us laugh or brought us joy. That's how they want to be remembered.

Spirits will give us signs that are unique or special to them, to identify that they are around us. If I were not at the lunch where Ed's spirit had a chance to talk to me as a medium who could hear him, he likely would have influenced the driver of someone who owns a similar vehicle to drive by the restaurant for Robert and Tom to notice and recall the funny memory.

That's how spirit works.

###

Chapter 8
Ed's Spirit Treasure Hunt:
How Mediumship Works

This chapter originally appeared in my book "Lessons Learned from Talking to the Dead."

Being a medium also means you have to be a detective, but the clues are usually difficult to decipher, so often they're overlooked or dismissed by the person for whom they are intended. For example, if a spirit stops a clock at the exact same time they died, which has happened often, a loved one could be quick to say, "The battery must've died." That's why I reply, "When it comes to spirit, there is no such thing as a coincidence."

In this chapter, you'll learn how paying attention to small things can sometime add up to something pretty incredible.

To start, I have to say that Ed provided me with one of the most incredible adventures that ever happened to me as a medium.

When Ed passed in December 1996, the cause and manner of death were suspicious. The mystery was solved in 2011 when Ed took me on a clue-filled journey to visit his family in Virginia. So many of Ed's messages during this adventure comforted and helped Ed's father overcome his grief.

This is the story of what I call Ed's "Spirit Treasure Hunt" and every time I tell this story it gives me chills.

How the Visit Started

Over the years, Tom kept in touch with Ed's father. In January 2011, we were putting away the Christmas cards we received the month before, one was from Ed's dad, whom I will call George.

We came up with an idea to visit George. I was excited because it would be my first time meeting anyone related to Ed. So, we contacted George and discussed some of the signs that Ed had already given me to prove that he's around us. George found them fascinating. He agreed that it would be great to see Tom again and meet me, especially since I was able to channel his late son.

We made a plan to visit in March 2011. I figured that Ed was listening because spirits can hear us and even hear our thoughts. What I didn't know is that our plan would inspire Ed to chat with me a lot before our visit. In fact, he was quite busy over the course of several weeks leading up to the trip.

Ed Puts a Plan in Action

Spirit has to work hard to make things line up. Here's what Ed had to do in order for me to get a book that wound up having personal significance to him. You'll find out how the book came into play near the end of the chapter. What you need to know here is that Ed's spirit basically led me to it.

The weekend before we left for Virginia, we were out and about, running our usual errands. It also happened to be the last weekend that a bookstore in our area would be opened, as the national chain had declared bankruptcy and was liquidating its assets. I told Tom that I felt an urge to stop and go inside. I now know it was Ed urging me to stop because he had an idea in his spirit brain. I remember thinking that I really didn't need another book, as I had a stack back at the house that I still had to read.

Tom remained in the truck while I walked through the remaining inventory. An hour went by and I didn't realize it. I started looking at mystery novels, then graphic superhero novels. When I didn't see anything, I felt a nudge to walk to the left side of the store. I didn't know what was there, I just went with it.

I was drawn to a large bookcase positioned against a wall, and when I looked at the subject matter of books, I took note of the category: "Spiritual and Paranormal." I thought, "Okay, those interest me, so I'll take a look."

I wasn't thinking of any book in particular, so I just flipped through them. Only one book in the entire section appealed enough for me to buy it. I had never even heard of the book.

When I returned to the pick-up truck, Tom looked at the small paperback book and asked, "You were in there all that time, and that was all you bought?" At that time, we didn't know how truly special that book would become.

When we went on our trip, I brought the book with me, but left it at the hotel when we met George. Keep this in mind for the big reveal.

Ed Stresses a "Jingle" and a Book

Ed provided me with words, pictures, and messages that didn't make sense to me until I connected with several living people who were close to him when he was alive. The day before we left for the trip, I was in the bathroom shaving and I felt his presence. Fortunately, spirits can fit even in small bathrooms.

It was a Friday morning and my mind was racing with thoughts of what I needed to accomplish that day. I was trying not to be distracted because I was already running behind, and needed to get to work. But Ed didn't care about my schedule. He thought of another personal thing that he wanted to share with me. One that would let his family know he is still very much around them today.

So, I asked Ed, "Alright. What's Up? What do you need from me, Ed?" He didn't reply audibly, but I heard him loud and clear. Spirits usually communicate with me telepathically, and this is exactly what Ed was doing. Ed repeated the word "jingle" several times. He inferred that it was personal and it meant something special. I couldn't imagine how in the world the word "jingle" could ever be something personal.

The next thing Ed told me was he dad needs to *"Get the book."* In my mind, Ed showed me a blue-jacketed book and indicated it was important. He stressed that the blue book was a message that *I needed to give to his father.*

I said to Ed, "Is that it? You tell me about a jingle and urge me to get some blue book and then disappear?" How does that help me? It didn't matter. He was done talking until the next clue.

The Strange Rowboat/Kayak

The next message Ed gave me made no sense to me at all… until we met Ed's brother later on.

Ed told me to focus as he showed me images of what looked like a rowboat on the side of a river or lake. However, he kept saying, "But, it's also a kayak." I pondered this message because I was unsure *how a rowboat could be considered a kayak*, but we would later know how that was possible.

I've learned to just write things down and trust the messages. Spirits know exactly what they're trying to convey and why. It's up to us to put the puzzle together.

A "Royal" Message

Some messages from spirit can be strange and disjointed, as with the rowboat/kayak message. Ed gave me more to think about when I heard him relate the words, "It's like a *duke or duchess."* He was making me think of royalty for some reason. I thought, "Ed came from Lynchburg, Virginia, and I was pretty sure that there were no royalty living there when he was growing up." Tom certainly never told me if Ed had met a member of a royal family. I was left to wonder what his cryptic message meant.

I started to get the sense that Ed thought it was fun to give me these crazy clues. It was almost as if he was having a good time trying to get me to figure out the personal nature of these odd puzzle pieces. That fun side of his personality was coming through, loud and clear, so it would make sense. Of course, as a spirit, he also knows I love reading mysteries, so if he was trying to wrap me into a mystery about him, he succeeded.

Although we would not be able to confirm the royal message's meaning during our visit, it became clear later.

Ed said his that his father needed to "turn on his computer and look through it to help confirm that his passing was an accident." I learned that George still had Ed's computer but couldn't get into it because it was password protected. Unfortunately, to this day, George still cannot get into the computer, but it didn't matter as Ed's messages unfolded into the truth.

Before arriving in Lynchburg, we stopped for an early dinner before continuing on the drive. While in the restaurant, I related to Tom all of Ed's messages. Since they had been partners for 9 years, perhaps some of the messages would trigger a memory and maybe he could make sense of them. But he couldn't. So we wrote down all of the messages on a paper napkin to make sure that we could recall them all in our conversations with George. All of these strange mysteries would be solved later.

Dinnertime! Ed's Here!

On March 18 we headed to the Chestnut Hill Bed and Breakfast in Orange, Virginia, where we stayed during our visit with George.

After we checked in, we decided to go to dinner and found the Silk Mill Restaurant. During dinner we were joined by Ed's spirit. It was no surprise that he showed up. He knew we were going to visit his dad because he had been talking to me for the two weeks beforehand.

It seemed that Ed really wanted in on our conversation. After all, we were talking about him so why wouldn't he want to listen? Just like people living in the physical world, we often want to know what others are saying about us. It's the same with spirits. Of course they want to know what you think of them. So, be careful about what you say about those who have passed. They can hear you!

As I sat at the table, Ed's spirit was fidgeting. He was acting like a little kid that couldn't sit still. I could feel his excitement. He was anxious to use my abilities to finally be able to talk with his dad after 15 years on the other side.

Over the course of dinner, Ed's feelings progressed from excitement and anxiety to love. In fact, the love was so strong that I began to get overcome with emotion. My eyes began to tear up. I thought "How strange it is to be talking with a living person, and a spirit fills you up with an emotion to the point where you feel as if you're shaking inside and your eyes tear up." But spirits share emotions, memories and even physical pain, so it was to be expected.

The Pharmacy and Soda Fountain

Ed wasn't done with his puzzle pieces, however. As dinner was wrapping up, Ed showed me an image of a 1950s-style soda fountain at a lunch counter inside a pharmacy. I wondered why Ed was showing me that image because he had been born in 1960.

Again, a medium's job isn't to guess the reason, it's just to present the image or the message. The message needs to be interpreted by the intended receiver. I've learned that it's never good to read into things, because it can set me off in the wrong direction.

I told Tom what Ed was showing me, and Tom replied that Ed's dad had been a pharmacist, so perhaps the soda fountain reference had to do with George's place of employment. I thought that made sense, but there had to be something more to it. The soda fountain reference must have something to do with an event that had recently taken place. It was something that Ed's spirit recently witnessed.

That old soda fountain became just another item to add to the growing list of references that we had to discuss with George.

Like all of the other signs he gave me, that, too, would become clear.

Ed's Cemetery Rendezvous

The next day we drove to the cemetery where Ed was buried; we made a plan to meet George there. It was a sunny day, with a clear blue sky. When we arrived at the cemetery, we parked on the road closest to Ed's plot. It didn't take long for Ed's spirit to show up.

(Photo: Ed's gravesite in Virginia. Credit: R. Gutro)

I immediately developed my characteristic headache that identifies when a spirit or ghost was present. Ed showed up because several of us had gathered to honor him. As soon as he strolled into the cemetery, the love *I felt from Ed's spirit was overwhelming.*

I felt Ed touch my left shoulder; it felt like the impression made by a cold hand. He had drawn energy from the motion of air molecules to manifest his presence, and by doing so, slowed the molecules down, cooling the air where he stood. With Ed's hand on my shoulder, I stood still for a moment.

Tom had already walked over to the grave, while I remained by the road. I told Tom that Ed was standing behind me with his hand on my shoulder.

Moments later we were joined by Ed's father. That was the first time I met George in person.

George knew of my abilities as a medium. In my first book, *Ghosts and Spirits*, I wrote about the first signs from Ed, and George had read the book.

After greeting each other with a hug, George and Tom looked down at Ed's grave site and began talking about him. That's when Ed poked me on my back. Ed told me to say out loud, "I'm not down there, I'm standing right next to you."

George and Tom shot me a look. They understood that I was talking on Ed's behalf. That was an emotional moment, and George decided to break the emotion with a laugh.

George always said to make sure he never buried in a cow pasture. Well this certainly resembles a cow pasture." It was a welcome break to the emotion of the moment.

We left the cemetery and followed George back to his house. Once settled on the couch, I pulled out the napkin with the list of references written on it. George was intrigued.

I read the list of references out loud. Some of them were immediately identified while others were left unresolved...for now.

The references that George couldn't identify immediately were the kayak/rowboat, jingle, "duke" or "duchess," and the blue book. George noted that he had a bunch of Ed's books stored in the basement, so he would check through them to see if one had any special meaning.

Ed Reveals his Spiritual Company

Because I never knew Ed in the physical or met his family before, I had no idea what he called people. That includes not knowing any nicknames he had for people, unless it was a nickname for Tom, which he freely seemed to tell me to be funny or annoying.

For that reason, what happened next was amazing, although it meant little to George and Tom. As we continued to talk to George in his living room, I sensed Ed walk into the room again. He sat next to me.

The next thing Ed said to me was "tell them I'm with Granny." Having grown up in Boston, I never referred to any of my grandmothers as "Granny" and I don't think I've ever met anyone use the term. In fact, the only time I remember hearing that word is when watching the Beverly Hillbilly's television program in the 1970s. So, it was unusual for me to hear that word.

In spite of that, I asked George if Ed ever referred to his grandmother as "Granny." George said, "Yes, Ed called my mother "Granny."

What's more, "Granny" had passed away the year before our trip. So why was Ed telling us he was with Granny? He simply wanted to let his dad know they were together on the other side.

I later learned that Ed had passed while staying in his Granny's house and that they had a very strong connection, so it makes sense that Ed would bring her up.

Mystery Solved: How Ed Really Passed

I learned that one of the most difficult parts of Ed's passing for his family and friends was the question of whether or not he took his own life.

It was suspected that Ed may have committed suicide. As with any suicide, the idea that someone took their own life often causes the victim's living friends and family to feel somehow personally responsible for the passing. Surviving friends and family often deal with guilt and ask what they could have done differently to prevent the tragic event. The true answer is that there is nothing they could have done.

So, the idea that anyone may have taken his or her own life just adds to the deep sense of loss already being felt by the living. Ed's dad had endured that double sense of loss for 15 years. Now, Ed wanted to bring some healing.

People who knew Ed thought of him as intelligent, funny, hardworking, and someone who enjoyed people. In addition to managing his own landscaping business, he used to read Grey's Anatomy just because he found it fascinating, and enjoyed Scrooge McDuck comic books, so he could be serious and be light-hearted. As a child, his father played classical music, so Ed grew up thinking the long dead composers were still alive, and that the music was contemporary. As he grew older, they would often play "Name That Tune" while listening to classical music stations.

Given his personality and life motivations, it was difficult to imagine that he would want to end it. In fact, George said when they found Ed, he was wearing a set of headphones and an open calendar of landscaping appointments was laying open by his side on the bed.

As I sat in the recliner in George's living room, having just told him that Ed is with Granny in the afterlife, Ed had another big message for me to pass along to his dad. It was about his death.

I heard Ed in my head, and repeated the words to George. "It was an accident." I then conveyed exactly what Ed was showing me in my mind, to help prove that his passing was accidental.

I told George that I saw an image of Heath Ledger, the actor who played a gay cowboy in the film "Brokeback Mountain," and "the Joker" in the 2008 film "The Dark Knight," about the DC Comics character, Batman.

Spirits will show us famous people that we can identify to understand something they're trying to tell us. What's interesting here is that Ed passed in December 1996. Heath Ledger's first film was *Blackrock* in 1997. So, Ledger wasn't even known as an actor in the U.S. when Ed died. That means that Ed is still very much aware of things that have transpired after he passed, and the reason is that he is connected with those of us still living in the physical world.

The New York Times reported that an initial autopsy on January 23, 2008 and a subsequent complete toxicological analysis was conducted on Ledger. The report concluded, in part, "Mr. Heath Ledger died as the result of acute intoxication by the combined effects of oxycodone, hydrocodone, diazepam, temazepam, alprazolam and doxylamine." It states definitively: "We have concluded that the manner of death is accident, resulting from the abuse of prescribed medications."

I figured it out. Ed showed me a reference I understood to solve the mystery of Ed's own passing. The next thing I told George was "Ed's death was the result of an interaction of prescription medications." Ed also had me say, "I didn't mean it."

George realized the revelation made perfect sense. Today, we know that the prescription medications that caused Ed's passing cannot be taken together because of their lethal consequence; required warning labels are the result. This was not the case in 1996.

George told me he could finally stop grieving so intensely because the cloud of suicide had been lifted. He took great comfort in finally learning the truth, as anyone would. He had been grieving for 15 years and thinking that Ed may have purposely taken his own life. "I knew it," his father said.

Meeting at the Soda Fountain

After that incredible message we decided to take a ride into the downtown area for lunch. George insisted on driving and giving us a tour; we gratefully accepted.

George told me that he would take us to lunch at a place that will solve another one of those puzzle pieces. He pulled his car up along the curb and parked in front of a building that had once been a drugstore but was now a sandwich shop.

George told us that as a young man, he had worked as a "soda jerk" at the very same drugstore's lunch counter many years ago.

(Photo: The former pharmacy, now restaurant where George reunited with other "Soda fountain jerks." Credit: R. Gutro)

That's when George told us that only days before our visit, he had lunch with some of his old friends, all of whom had worked as soda jerks in the very same drugstore; a small reunion of sorts.

Now it all made sense to me. Ed showed me the image of the soda fountain because he had been there listening to the conversation his dad was having with his old friends earlier that week.

Solving the Weird Rowboat/Kayak Puzzle

Over lunch we continued to recall the remaining signs, like the duke/duchess combination, the mysterious book with the light blue cover, and the combination rowboat/kayak hybrid. We could come up with no answers for any of them, but knew they must mean something to someone.

After lunch George decided it would be nice to introduce me to his other son, Ed's brother, David. Tom had known David for many years. So, after a call to ensure David and his family would be home, we were off again.

As we pulled up to Dave's house we immediately noticed a boat on trailer hitch sitting in the driveway. The boat was covered with a canvas. As George parked his car at the end of the driveway, he looked at Tom and I and said "Let's see what this means."

I had never met Dave before, and he certainly didn't know about my abilities as a medium. George also never told Dave about any of the previous messages from Ed that we had been discussing.

We got out of the car as Dave came out of the house to greet us. As he approached the car, Dave gestured toward the boat and asked, "What do you think of my new boat?" He had only just purchased it two weeks before and had it shipped from Colorado, right about the same time that Ed's spirit conveyed the rowboat/kayak message to me.

The next thing Dave said stopped us in our tracks. "I've already enjoy rowing it out on the lake and fishing with it," he said. I thought to myself, "This may be the rowboat that Ed was telling me about, but what about the kayak?"

After we went inside and met Dave's wife and children, it was as we were leaving that we learned about the kayak part of the puzzle.

I remember that George had already made it down the stairs to the walkway, Tom was a couple of steps from the bottom, and I was behind him, when Dave glanced at his rowboat and said, "Although it's a rowboat, it has a flat bottom. And because you steer it with oars, and it's made of fiberglass, it's kind of like a kayak."

So this was the rowboat/kayak combination that Ed showed me but I didn't understand. I also didn't say anything about it because I was unsure if Dave believed in spirits. Tom and I looked at each other wide-eyed and didn't say a word.

It seemed like time stopped for a moment. Tom and I looked at each other wide-eyed and didn't say a word. That new boat was indeed the "rowboat/kayak."

Dave caught the non-verbal exchange between us and asked, "Have you guys ever been kayaking?" I quickly related our kayak excursion to a bioluminescent bay in Puerto Rico. I didn't want to freak Dave out by telling him that his dead brother knew about the boat purchase and had even been out with him fishing in the lake.

I'll also never forget George's reaction. He was nearest to the car when Dave mentioned the kayak and George stopped in his tracks. He looked as shocked as Tom and I did, and quickly said, "We have to go."

As we drove off, George couldn't stop talking about it. "Did you hear that?" he asked. "It's both a rowboat and a kayak. How crazy is that?" If I hadn't heard it myself, I likely would not have believed Ed's crazy message actually made sense.

This is yet another instance of Ed's spirit being around a member of his family the week or two prior to our visit. It holds true for everyone reading this book: the spirits of your loved ones are around you from time to time, especially during significant life events - like buying a new boat.

Residual Energy to the Touch

Our next destination was to see the last vehicle that Ed owned. In the mid-1990s, Ed bought white Toyota pickup truck. After he passed, Dave was given the vehicle, making it well over 15 years old by the time of our visit. The truck was parked in front of Dave's commercial garage, and of course, it was still in perfect running condition, since Dave had put a new engine in it and replaced the clutch.

As a medium, touching something that once belonged to a person who has passed, sometimes provides insight into the spirit's personality, memories, or past actions. That's because whenever someone owns a possession, an item they were attached to in life, they leave behind residual energy, an "imprint" on it.

(Photo: Ed's pick-up truck from the 1990s. Photo: R. Gutro)

Residual energy is like an emotional thumbprint that someone living can leave on an object or in a place they dwelled. When a living person comes in contact with the object, they bring their own energy that enhances the residual energy on the object. In essence, a living person acts as a battery to "power up" the imprint of emotions that were left on an object. As such, the living person may feel the emotions attached to the object.

When we arrived at the garage, I could immediately tell which truck was Ed's, because it was white and it appeared old, not because I know anything about vehicles.

It was no surprise to me that when I touched the pick-up truck that I was flooded with residual energy of his love for the truck. It also felt like a warm blanket on a cold day, embracing me with love. Although I didn't get any visual or memory implant, the emotion remained.

Sensing Residual Energy

As a medium, I've sensed residual energy on pieces of furniture, and in homes. You can also find very emotional residual energies in hospitals or abandoned prisons. Those are places that have residual hauntings where events replay over and over.

The difference between residual energy and intelligent energy, is that intelligent energy or hauntings (in the case of a ghost or a spirit) means that the entity can communicate with you and answer questions. Residual energy doesn't have an intelligence and can't answer questions.

Everyone has the ability to sense residual energy. For example, if you go into an old home, and feel anxious or nervous, you may be sensing the residual energy imprinted upon the walls from a bad or traumatic emotional event. Conversely, you may feel a sense of peace when you go into a different room, where someone enjoyed relaxing or entertaining friends.

Residual energy is an imprint of an emotional reaction from living people in the past. Anyone can sense them, but mediums just have a heightened sense of the energy.

"Jingle" Finally Rings a Bell

After we visited Ed's truck, we got back into George's car and headed back to George's house. On the ride back, George exclaimed, "I know what "jingle" means."

When we arrived at George's house, we couldn't get out of the car fast enough. George unlocked the front door of the house and quickly walked to a room where Ed's belongings were being stored.

He retrieved a container that Ed used to keep loose change, an old coffee tin, wrapped in a paper sleeve, a homemade arts-and-crafts project that had been a gift from two of his old college friends, who were now graphic artists. The sleeve read, "Jingle Java."

This is the "jingle" that had a special meaning for Ed because he used it every day, filling the tin container with coins.

When I initially heard Ed say over and over the word "jingle" to me, I thought it might be a reference to the Christmas holidays. I had no inkling that it might actually refer to coins. This is a perfect illustration of why mediums should never try to be the interpreter of the messages they receive from spirit, but rather only act as the conduit to relate the messages to the intended recipient, and let them decipher the messages.

This was yet another out-of-the-blue sign from Ed with a perfectly personal explanation. I was again in awe of the messages Ed was conveying and how these random images and words were making total sense to his family.

(PHOTO: Ed's "Jingle Java" coin can. Credit: R. Gutro)

Blue Book Search Continues

After the "Jingle Java" revelation, we focused on the last couple of Ed's mysterious signs that remained unsolved. We started with the blue book.

As we stood in the room filled with Ed's belongings, among them were several boxes of books.

We combed through the boxes, hoping to discover the meaning of the blue book. When a spirit gives you something as general as a "blue book" it can be difficult to know exactly what you are looking for.

Tom found one of Ed's uncompleted poems inserted between the pages of a book of poetry by Walt Whitman, but the book's cover wasn't blue, so that wasn't it. We continued to search through the boxes of books, and not one had a blue cover. I couldn't understand what Ed was trying to bring to our attention. We were puzzled and decided that we would hopefully figure it out later.

We also couldn't decipher the meanings of "Duke or Duchess." The meaning of that message would also come later.

A Spirit-directed Hug

As a medium, I sense energy, emotions, and physical sensations from spirits. They often get excited when they know I'm able to convey messages to their living loved ones.

As we were leaving, Ed's spirit approached me for the last time while I was in the presence of his dad. I clearly heard Ed tell me, "Please hug my dad, and tell him it's from me."

The logical thinker in me thought, "I only just met George today, and it may not be appropriate to hug him."

Ed was adamant that I give his dad a hug, so I said, "Ed wants me to give you a hug." George understood. As I hugged George goodbye, it was very emotional for me. I felt Ed was using me to give his dad one more hug from him. We now have a special bond that didn't exist before this trip and for which I'm forever grateful.

Blue Book Puzzle Solved One Week Later

After we returned home, the two unsolved messages from the list would soon be solved: the "blue book" and the words "duke or duchess." We received a letter in the mail from George with answers that surprised us all.

Tom started reading the letter out loud. George wrote:

"I think I may have a connection on the "Blue Book" and "Duke/Duchess." See what you think.

First the book. Thinking about the story of Cornelia Clopton and her appearance 50 years later in her former house, I know that somewhere I had that story by a local newspaper columnist which I clipped from the paper.

I was looking around downstairs when I happened to look through a book in which I had stuck some things years ago. This book had been sent to me by a cousin just after Ed died. (This cousin had lost his 19 year old daughter some years earlier and it was her memorial bench there at the cemetery where we met [last week]).

The book is a collection of stories recounting after-death contact and experiences by people who had lost loved ones. I also put in the book 4 accounts by my cousin of his encounters with his deceased daughter and I had been wondering where they might be.

This book was a life-saver for me at that time and I kept it close to me and read and re-read it constantly for 2 or 3 years. It brought me great comfort and was an emotional life preserver. It is standard size and of 350 pages. Front and back covers are blue, as well as the cover jacket."

I immediately jumped up from the table. "Stop!" I told Tom. I ran upstairs, leaving Tom sitting at the table calling to me, "What are you doing? Where are you going?"

I had this urge to run upstairs to retrieve the book I was currently reading. Once I had the book in my hand I returned to the kitchen table and I said to Tom, "Okay, now you can go on."

Tom said, "Ed's dad sent a photo of the book's front cover," and as he turned over the photograph, I laid down the book on the table. They were the VERY SAME BOOK. Tom and I looked at each other in surprise.

Tom looked back down at the letter and continued reading it. *"The title of the book is Hello from Heaven. Above the title are the words "Have you been contacted by a loved one who has died?" I enclose a photo."* This was indeed the blue book Ed wanted his father to find.

There are two important takeaways from this amazing sign. First, Ed wanted his dad to read the book again to get comfort from the messages from others in spirit.

Second, it was Ed who inspired me to stop at the Border's Bookstore the weekend before our trip. It was Ed who led me to pick that particular book out in the entire store, so that we would know what "blue book" he was talking about! Ed led me to the exact same book 15 years after it helped his dad cope with grief when Ed passed. That blue book was such an intense, personal message that Ed was indeed around his family.

Just think of all the millions of books in print. I bought the exact same, obscure 16 year old book that had actually helped Ed's dad work through his grief in 1996. Unbelievable, but true! It was all because of Ed in spirit, leading me to find and buy that book.

There's another part to this story that is of interest. I had taken that book with me on our trip to visit George, but left it in the hotel room. If I had brought it with me during our visit, George would have immediately recognized it, and the impact of the message would have been lost. So, Ed had to work twice as hard to get his dad to remember that particular book.

The bottom line is that there is no such thing as a coincidence when it comes to spirit.

Deciphering the Royal Message

Ed's father's letter next addressed the message of "duke and duchess" that I received and we couldn't figure out during our visit. Ed's dad's letter continued:

"The impression Rob received of "Duke" or "Duchess" may well be "Count" or "Countess."

If you recall during our tour around town, I stopped very briefly in front of a home across from the beautiful mansion called "Villa Maria." I mentioned, off-handedly, that it was once the residence of Countess Raffalovich and that Eleanor Roosevelt had visited here. None of us seemed to catch it at the time and we moved quickly on in our whirlwind tour of the town.

My sister has a recipe for Countess Raffalovich's spaghetti and ever since I moved back to town in 1998, my sister has invited us over every 2 or 3 months to have a spaghetti dinner. "Countess Raffalovich's spaghetti" has long been a common expression among us.

About 2 weeks ago, my sister was exulting over her new dishwasher and I said "Well, you will have to fix the Countess Raffalovich's spaghetti and invite me over so we can dirty some dishes."

Ed's dad went on to say how I was likely interpreting "duchess" as "countess" which makes perfect sense. So, what does it mean? It means that Ed's spirit was there when his dad was talking about being invited over for "Countess Raffalovich's spaghetti."

Sometimes the signs that spirits give us may not be obvious, but usually over a short period of time, they become apparent, just as every sign that Ed's spirit gave me made sense.

After-thoughts from the Spirit Treasure Hunt

This journey serves as a perfect example of how signs, words, messages, and symbols that a medium receives from a loved one may not be immediately apparent or obvious to the recipient. Some investigation may be necessary to make sense of them. There are reasons why a spirit chooses to convey messages in a certain way, in a certain order, or with very specifically chosen words or images; it is their way of making the confirmation very personal to the one left behind.

The most rewarding part of this "Spirit Treasure Hunt" was that Ed's dad was finally able to find a way to cope with his immeasurable loss. After more than 15 years, Ed showed his dad that he's still around his family. It brought peace to his dad, Tom, and to me. What's interesting is that even though I never met Ed while he was alive in the physical world, I've grown to know and love him in spirit as a close, personal friend.

As I've said to Tom, "It was really awesome taking a vacation with you. And Ed."

###

Chapter 9
Ed Finally Adopts a Dog

This chapter originally appeared in my book "Pets and the Afterlife."

Ed always wanted a dog but never got to adopt one. When our dog, Sprite, passed in 2013, Tom revealed to me Ed's wish for a canine companion.

In 2005, my dog, Buzz, passed, but that was before I knew Tom (or Ed in spirit). I had just assumed that Buzz and Ed had found each other in spirit. In 2013, we had to make the awful decision to assist our elderly dog Sprite pass. Ed became an important part in helping us heal from the resultant grief and sense of loss we experienced.

This chapter addresses the situation that many pet owners either have or will confront, choosing to help beloved pets pass. I also offer a way to help understand that you made the proper choice and that guilt should never factor into the equation, because it's all done out of love and compassion.

This chapter will help with understanding that your beloved pet is safely with the spirits of loved ones and capable of communicating from the other side.

Why Signs from Spirit Take a While

Everyone wants to get a message or a sign from someone who passed, whether it is a pet or a person. However, those signs are usually blocked because of grief. When that happens and you need healing, I recommend consulting with a medium, or perhaps even a Master of Reiki. They will better be able to connect to spirit for you because they are not dealing with the personal grief.

However, once a spirit crosses over into the light, it takes a lot of energy for them to come back. An analogy would be it's similar to biking up a steep hill. Once all that energy has been expended to reach the top, time is required to rest and recover from that exertion in order to fully function again.

I am very fortunate to count other mediums among my closest friends, and during my time of grieving all of them contacted me and conveyed very similar messages from our beloved pet that had recently departed.

While I'm addressing the passing of a pet in this chapter, I want to reiterate an important part of dealing with the decision to let them go. So many people suffer from second thoughts and guilt after helping their pets cross over. Since it's on topic, and so many households have pets I thought this would be worth repeating from my *Pets and the Afterlife* book.

When is "the Right Time"?

Every resource I've read acknowledged that knowing when to let go of a beloved pet is an extremely intense and deeply personal decision. The tendency to second guess the decision to put down a pet is a normal part of the grieving process; feelings of grief can easily migrate into feelings of guilt. Although it's natural to have these mixed feelings, we need to remind ourselves that our pets cannot tell us when they are experiencing pain and are ready to go.

Such feelings and emotions are exactly what we experienced when making the decision to let go of our Dachshund, Sprite, whose quality of life rapidly diminished in a very short period of time.

Sprite's Story

In early December, 2010, Sprite came to us as a foster through a local Dachshund rescue. He was just a few weeks shy of turning 14 years old. Sprite had been surrendered after his owners, an elderly couple, both passed within months of each other, and the other family members didn't want to care for a senior dachshund.

Sprite was not housetrained. We learned that he had not been to a vet since 2006, and required all of the usual routine shots and tests. Other required medical procedures included neutering, the extraction of 22 rotted teeth, and removal of a large tumor-like growth from under his chin.

Our vet also informed us of Sprite's irregular heartbeat. With that diagnosis, options for treatment of future ailments would be severely limited; for example, he could no longer be anesthetized. She also cautioned that if he were adopted out, that the stress of adapting to yet another new home environment could be potentially fatal. So in mid-2011, we decided to adopt Sprite and expand our brood of canines.

Sprite was not accustomed to being hugged, and would release a little grunt under his breath when squeezed. He never returned affection, such as giving us "kisses" – which was probably a good thing because of his rancid breath. He never played with toys, nor engaged in tug-of-war or other games with our other dogs. It wasn't until December 2012, just about two years later, that Sprite finally began to approach me for head rubs, or greet us at the door when we came home.

Sprite eventually bonded with our other dogs, and we were a contented three-dog family. But in 2012, Sprite's health began to decline marked by the loss of sight in one eye, and diminished vision in the other. His hearing also declined, and his kidneys began to fail as evidenced by his inability to retain urine. In the first half of 2013, we began to ponder whether Sprite's time with us was rapidly drawing to a close.

During the first week in July, he was having difficulty using his back legs. I decided I would watch him closely that week, and wound up picking him up and carrying him outside. I knew time was drawing near to make the agonizing decision.

On the evening of July 7, around 9:30 p.m., Sprite developed an uncontrollable nose bleed. The bleeding became profuse and would not clot; the flow of blood caused him to sneeze. At 10:30 p.m., his breathing became labored so I took him to the emergency vet's office. Sprite responded to treatment after 30-45 minutes, and the vet successfully managed to control the bleeding.

(Sprite in 2011. Credit: R. Gutro)

The new diagnosis, however, was that Sprite had possibly developed a tumor in the nasal cavity. The testing for a tumor required that he be put under anesthesia, which was not an option because of his heart murmur.

Because of his lengthy list of other ailments, it was at this time the emergency vet asked if I wanted to euthanize him that night. I refused. If Sprite's time to pass was drawing near, I wanted him to be at home, with all of us together one last time.

Asking for Spiritual Help

The spirits of our loved ones are always waiting to greet us (and our pets) on the other side. There are countless accounts of people who, in their final hours, are seen speaking to someone or something not visible to us, possibly someone waiting for them in the light. That's because dying and leaving the physical body can be a scary thing for almost everyone. Our loved ones in spirit want to reassure us that they are indeed present to guide us and keep us safe.

That said, I called on Ed, my dad who passed in 2008, and Buzz, my dog who passed in 2005, to be there waiting for Sprite when we took him to the veterinarian's office for that final visit.

I remember carrying Sprite from the car into the vet's office and waiting in the lobby for a couple of minutes. I was too distraught to sense if my request for help had been regarded.

Once Tom and I were brought into one of the exam rooms, we conferred with the doctor who explained the process. Sprite was really out of it. He was so tired, and his energy was gone. It was obvious he was ready to go.

The doctor provided a sedative and then left us in the room with Sprite for a couple of minutes while the medication took effect. As soon as we were alone in the room, I realized that all of the spirits I asked for help had arrived.

It was July and hot outside, so I was wearing a short-sleeved tee shirt. I remember that because I suddenly felt a hand lightly grip the back of my arms. It was a cool sensation. I realized that Ed was standing to my left side, between Tom and I, and my dad was standing to my right side. Both were holding my elbows in their hands to let me know they were there. It was comforting and very emotional.

I glanced to my right and looked at the floor, and sitting there, in the "sit" position was Buzz in spirit. My dad and Ed had brought Buzz with them as I had requested. Buzz was going to help Sprite cross over into the light.

The Moment

On July 8, 2013, at 5:50 p.m., Tom and I said goodbye to our oldest canine boy. Our veterinarian was so compassionate and caring. She explained about the second injection as she administered it and we held onto Sprite's little front paws. We had wrapped him in his favorite blanket as Tom and I, the veterinarian, Ed, my dad and Buzz surrounded him. Little Sprite passed peacefully.

As the words, "His heart has stopped" were spoken, such a sense of finality was conveyed that the flow of tears could not be stopped. After a few moments alone with him, the vet entered the room and gingerly removed the limp body. That was the last we saw of our Sprite in the physical form until we received his ashes in a box.

Moving On

As we stood in the room trying to acknowledge what happened, Ed, my dad, and Buzz were no longer there. They had come for Sprite, and Sprite left with them.

Although I knew Sprite left with them, I still wanted proof they were together. Everyone wants reassurances that their loved ones are okay in spirit, and since I was so heavy in grief, I didn't see Sprite's spirit cross over (although I knew he did) so I wanted proof. Ed and my dad would provide that proof soon enough.

The Questioning

I'm going to interrupt Ed's story with Sprite again to address the questioning that happens after euthanizing a pet. It's something that happens often, and it happened to me. The feelings of guilt and tendency to second guess the decision made can be overwhelming.

A couple of days after Sprite passed, I responded to a friend's email by recounting my observations of Sprite's health that led to our decision.

If you are a pet owner, I urge you to do the same. Email a friend, tell them in detail what you have observed, and ask for an impartial opinion. Then read it over and over again. Once I read the email that I sent to our friend, I realized that it had been the right thing to do, and it had been the right time to let Sprite pass. The following is my email to our friend Merle:

Date: Wed, 10 Jul 2013
Hi Merle - We are still questioning if we did the right thing with Sprite. I've gone over this a hundred times already. I'm writing these things down to help us understand that it was best for him.
- We knew Sprite was failing last year when he couldn't walk around the neighborhood anymore.
- We knew he had a bad heart murmur and his kidney failure really became bad around January, when he had to go out every 5 hours or so, and immediately after he ate and drank.
- I put towels down in the kitchen for him overnight, and I know he felt badly every time he peed in the house.
- Last week, he couldn't even get up and peed on his bed and blanket.
- His little back legs were weak, and for the last 6 months I've had to carry him up and downstairs. In the last couple of months I've had to carry him outside, and sometimes back inside (he couldn't get strength in his back legs and his muscles were wasting).
- Our friend, Yolie let the dogs out this weekend and had to pick him up and bring him outside, too.
- He was blind in one eye, and could only see light and shadows in the other.
- He walked into walls and doors.
- He was going deaf, too.
- Last week he stopped eating his kibble and the wet food. He would only eat treats.
- After Sunday night in the Emergency Room, the vet there said that his 2 1/2 hour nosebleed could be from a tumor and any tests would require putting him out- which would've killed

him. She said they stopped the bleeding, but couldn't promise it wouldn't return.

- He stopped holding his tail up in the air. His tail used to always stay pointed up, and wagged all the time.

- Another indicator was when he stopped being engaged, and would wander off and sit facing a wall for hours at a time. It was almost like he had "checked out" on living.

Taking into account all of these things, and the lack of interest in dinner (which has never happened), Sprite looked old and tired and worn out. We thought that with the bleeding possibility and everything else, that it was time. I just hope we were right.

After I sent this email, I read it over and over again, and it really helped me come to terms that we did the right thing at the right time for little Sprite. I recommend that any pet owner evaluate their pet's quality of life, and make a list if you have to, to determine if you're doing the right thing. As difficult as this time may be, it is important to remain strong for your beloved pet. Remember, they will be around you when it's your turn, as the next part of this story proves.

Another Medium Confirms Ed's Presence

In my *Pets and the Afterlife* book, I wrote about how Sprite's spirit came through to three different mediums I knew, and with similar messages. What's amazing is that those three mediums confirmed each other's messages from Sprite without knowing each other. They also confirmed some things that we were sensing. You can read about those messages in that book.

But one of the mediums knew that there were other spirits in the room when Sprite passed. That was my friend Ruthie Larkin (BeantownMedium.com).

Ruthie pinpointed a special blanket and identified the three spirits I asked to come into the vet's office with us when it was Sprite's time. There was no way she could know the exact three spirits that I was asking to help me. Further, she confirmed that they were there when I felt them in the vet's office. Here are the messages she received:

July 10, 2013 2:53 p.m. EDT
Ruthie called me. She said that Sprite came to her yesterday. She started writing this note, and had to call me today at 2:45 p.m. because as she was writing it, Sprite came back in!

July 10, 2013 14:51:31 -0400
From: Ruthie Larkin (www.beantownmedium.com)
To: Rob Gutro
Subject: HERE'S THE EMAIL WHERE I HAD TO STOP AND CALL YOU
Thank you Rob! I know you are grieving for your little Sprite and I appreciate you taking the time to interpret this photo for me. By the way, I thought of Sprite yesterday and when I did I saw him very clearly jumping around and in beautiful shape and very happy. You know I don't always get the pets but he came in very clear. In fact, he is showing me right [this is where she stopped writing]

Ruthie stopped writing and called me and said Sprite was jumping up and down, saying "thank you, thank you." He told her that he was actually in a lot of pain and his stiff legs hurt a lot and now he is finally free of pain. She said that his coat is shiny and bright, and he appears in full health, and is very grateful to us for making the choice.

Ruthie said (and later wrote this to me in an email so I would have it) *"Sprite sent you love through me 3 separate times. When a Spirit wants to send love they will fill every cell in my body with an unbelievable feeling that goes from my toes to the top of my head. You know how you will get chills when you receive confirmation from Spirit… well, this is 100 times better!!! I can barely say a word when it comes through and I always immediately know that my client (in this case Rob) is receiving a great deal of love from their deceased loved one."*

When Ruthie asked if Sprite was wrapped in a special blanket, I told her he was. We wrapped him in his favorite dark blanket at the vet's office. Ruthie said that Sprite wants that blanket around. I told her I was planning to put it under his ashes and she said that's perfect.

She also noted that Buzz is with him. She said: *"Buzz looks like a smaller dog, though, even though I thought he was a Weimaraner."* I told her that Buzz was a puppy when he passed.

She also validated what Tom said he felt about Ed. She said "Ed is very happy to be with Sprite and happy to finally have a dog." The night Sprite passed, Tom said, "I'm sure Ed is happy because he finally has the dog that I wouldn't let him have." Ruthie then told me that she also saw my Dad around Ed, Buzz and Sprite. She said that my Dad was also with them.

How Spirits Use Coins

Spirits will use items to give us confirmation of their presence. One of the most common ways they do that is through coins. As beings of energy, spirits can move lightweight objects from one place to another. Coins are an effective means of communicating because they contain a year.

Spirits will often try to find a coin near you that contains a year related to them, so the messenger will be easier to identify. So if you find a coin that has the year of someone's birth or the year of their passing, you will know which person in spirit sent it to you.

The most difficult part for a spirit is finding a coin that someone dropped with an appropriate year and moving it to a place you will find it. Just think of how much doing that takes!

There are many other vehicles that spirit can use, too. Feathers, flowers, and influencing living things to act erratically on special dates are various other methods spirits convey their presence. You'll find a more extensive list in my books *Ghosts and Spirits* or *Lessons Learned from Talking to the Dead.*

Spirits Later Confirm Sprite is With Them

After I asked the spirits of Ed, my dad and Buzz to help Sprite cross over in the vet's office, I asked them to give me proof. Days later, they gave me those confirmations.

One week after Sprite's passing, as Tom and I were getting out of our car, he found a penny. The penny was dated 1996, the year that Ed passed. Ed dropped that penny in front of Tom, so he would find it and understand that Sprite is with him now. It was also a confirmation that Ed was in the veterinarian's office when Sprite was transitioning.

It didn't take long for my dad to use the same method of communication. The next day, as I was getting out of my car at Dunkin' Donuts to get a morning coffee there was the sign. Laying on the ground, right outside of the driver's side car door was a shiny penny. When I picked it up, the year was 2008. That was the year my dad passed.

Dad had also sent me a sign that Sprite was also with him, Buzz and Ed.

Spirit Help: A Lesson to All

The most important thing to take from this story is that spirits of our loved ones will be there for us whenever we call on them. They want to help us through emotional times. They want to support us, and although we may not physically see them they'll confirm that they are indeed around. All we have to do is ask.

Sprite Signs

Since Sprite passed in 2013, from time to time have sensed him in the house. We can tell where he's walking around, or if he's just laying down watching us and our other four dogs. He still likes to sit by the front door and watch the cars go by outside, and that's sometimes where we see a little dark shadow.

Of course, every night before I go to bed, I always say goodnight to Sprite, Buzz, Ed and my parents. Spirits can hear us, and they enjoy being acknowledged.

###

Chapter 10
Ed's Birthday Wishes

I didn't document all the times that Ed came through in 2014, but one notable occurrence that stood out that year happened on Tom's birthday.

Previously I discussed how spirits use coins as a physical manifestation in this reality of their presence. Ed seems to prefer this methodology, which makes sense since one of his favorite possessions was the special bank that his co-workers made him with the "Jingle Java" label.

Just before Tom's birthday in November, Ed told me that he would be acknowledging the birthday. Although the passing or marking of time isn't really a "thing" of importance on the other side, he always marked the anniversary of Tom's birthday.

(Photo: Tom found a 1996 Penny. Credit: R.G)

Since we never know how Ed is going to appear, we kept our eyes open for anything. He had already appeared visibly to us riding in the back seat of my pickup truck, and another time he sent a look-like to help us when we became lost in the English countryside.

This year, though, he opted for his favorite method of communicating by sending a little "Jingle" or coin. During the week of Tom's birthday, he found a penny dated 1996, the year Ed passed.

That was a sign that Ed was wishing Tom a happy birthday from the afterlife, just as spirits of your loved ones will do for you.

###

Chapter 11
Ed Adopts Buzz

On February 22, 2015, ten years after the passing of my puppy, Buzz, Ed found a way to reassure me that Buzz was with him, as was our other dog, Sprite, whom also passed. The timing of the message provided the confirmation that they had indeed found each other in spirit.

In 2005, after Buzz passed, he immediately became the world's best canine spirit communicator. His numerous visitations made me aware of just how many ways were possible for a dog or cat to communicate with us from the other side.

Buzz taught me that pets in spirit can manipulate objects that use electrical power, guide us toward look-alikes, move items, and make audible noises such as the sound of barking or paw's nails on the floor. A favorite method of communication used by Buzz is to influence me to turn on the radio at a specific time to hear a song with a message of love from him. He also has moved coins and positioned them to be in my path, and influenced things in nature. He has shown me that pets can use many of the same signs that human spirits use to convey their presence.

Pet Spirits Understand Special Dates

Just as pets use many of the same vehicles to communicate their presence to the living, they also acknowledge the special days. Living pets read our energy and they sense heightened emotional energy from us on birthdays, anniversaries, holidays and special occasions, so they mark those dates in their memories. Of course, they can't read a calendar, but they can sense our emotional levels, as they elevate or drop, and read these as indications that a date of importance is pending.

In February, 2015, Buzz recruited Ed to make sure I knew that they found each other in spirit, and the Ed had "adopted" a second dog.

(Photo: Buzz on Oct. 30, 2004 at 3 months. Credit: R. Gutro)

Ask and You Will Receive

Spirits are a form of energy, and as such they can read thoughts and hear sound, which are also different forms of energy. Spirits also behave just like as they did when they were in the physical world. So, if you want them to help you with something, or let you know they are around you, just ask them.

On the night of February 11, I asked Buzz Wyatt to send a sign that he was around, and on, February 12, he responded.

During my lunch break that day, I drove to the post office to mail a package. I pulled the truck into an end parking space closest to a median. As I stepped out of the truck, I examined my parking job to make sure I hadn't parked too close to the curb that I would potentially scrape the tire rim backing out. I distinctly recall that there was nothing on the curb or in the grass of the median. I remember looking down to avoid tripping, and to ensure I didn't put my foot in the space between the truck and the curb.

I was inside the post office for only a few minutes. After mailing the package, I returned to the truck. And as I approached the driver's side door, shiny object on the curb caught my eye, the very same place I had looked when I stepped out of the truck. It was a nickel gleaming in the sunlight. When I saw it, I said to myself, "Hello, Edward." I just knew it was from him.

I confess that I thought it very odd because the nickel was definitely not on the ground when I initially parked and got out of the truck. But that's how spirits work.

When I crouched down and picked up the nickel, it was dated 1996, the year of Ed's passing. That confirmed that it was indeed from Ed.

In the short window of time that I had been inside the post office, Ed found a nickel and apported, or moved, it to the driver's side of my pick-up truck, where I was sure to see it. As soon as I read the year stamped on the nickel, I heard Ed say, "I've got my other dog, and I wanted to let you know." That was Ed's way of confirming that my dog, Buzz, was with him as was also Sprite who had passed in 2013.

(Photo: The nickel Ed sent. Credit: R. Gutro)

Ed used the coin with the date of his passing to convey he was with Buzz, on the anniversary month of Buzz's passing. I asked Ed for a sign that Buzz was with him and he happily provided it, through coins, one of his favorite methods of communication.

The lesson here is that you should always be vigilant for signs from spirit, especially around significant dates. Your people or pets in spirit will let you know they're around, especially if you ask them. We just have to be open-minded and pay attention to things around us and not dismiss them. There are no coincidences when it comes to spirit.

###

Chapter 12
Stop the Clock!

I've talked about how spirits are energy coupled with memories, personality, and knowledge. But as energy, they can manipulate things that run on energy. Once they store up enough of a charge, spirits can then communicate with the living.

Sources of energy used by spirits include heat, light, moving water, and electricity. For spirits who have crossed over the emotional energies of love, faith, and hope also provide sufficient energy for them to communicate. You will recall that earth-bound ghosts draw on negative emotional energies like fear, depression, anger and anxiety.

That said, if a possession that once belonged to a family member who passed is now in the home of loved ones, the spirit will likely use that object to communicate their presence. They do that by using the emotional energy of love once shared with them. That energy can help a spirit make a noise, play with electricity, move things, or even stop a clock.

Spirits and Clocks

Spirits have been known to use clocks in several ways. They can stop a clock, make it chime when it's not supposed to, or open a part of it, all in an effort to convey their presence. Often, people who are about to pass will leave their bodies and go to the home of their loved ones and stop a clock at the exact moment of their death. That's a very common way of letting their loved ones know they have passed.

Ed Clocks In

Although Ed didn't stop a clock, he did manipulate it. In mid-December 2015, we received a letter from Ed's sister-in-law that read, *"[The door to] Ed's [wall-mounted] clock was standing open yesterday—the first time since summer."* It had opened on its own. We know that Ed opened it to let his brother and sister-in-law know that he's very much around them.

(Photo: Ed's spirit opened the face of his mantle clock during the anniversary week of his passing.)

The clock was originally a Christmas gift from Tom to Ed. After Ed passed, the clock came into the possession of his brother's family.

The timing of the communication was not a coincidence. Ed opened the face of the clock on the anniversary week of his passing to reassure his brother's family that he's still very much around.

###

Chapter 13
Spirits Can Go Anywhere

As beings of energy, spirits can travel anywhere around the world or throughout the cosmos at any time. They can sit in your car and keep you company on the way to work. They can make sure that you're sleeping soundly and protect your house and family at night. They can appear in multiple places at the same time. As a medium, I have been unable to find the boundaries of their ability to be any place and time.

Several Places at the Same Time

People have asked me how spirits are able to be in two places at the same time. I believe that's possible because they are beings of energy with a consciousness. As a being of energy, they can split their energy and separate to attend to two or more living people at the same time.

Think of spirits as electricity coming from an electrical socket. If you plug in one light, the energy lights up one light. However, if you plug in a power strip and connect it to two lights, a computer and a television, that energy can get split up and appear in 4 different devices at the same time. That's basically what a spirit can do by dividing their energies.

That's how people who are dying have been able to contact multiple family members and friends anywhere in the world, at the time of their passing. The dying person's energy (that will become a spirit once crossed over) leaves the person's body as an astral projection, and is able to split up and tune into the energy of their loved ones to communicate with them.

Remember, the love we share with others acts as an "energy rope" that enables us to find each other on the other side.

Now that you know how they can go places and find you, Ed did that very thing when we took a vacation in England. Ed's spirit was with us throughout our entire 10-day vacation, and during that time, he gave us several signs so we would acknowledge his presence.

Ed's Jingle

Back in Chapter 8, you read about Ed's love of coins and his "Jingle Java" bank. The "jingle" or coins were one of Ed's favorite ways to communicate.

In 2013, part of our vacation in England took us to Bath. Dating from the first century A.D., the Romans built a sprawling bath complex using the thermally heated spring water found in the area. Although the baths had a lot of residual energy, Ed did not make his presence known. In fact, up to this point, I hadn't had any thoughts of Ed on our vacation.

(Photo: A 10 pence British coin. Credit: R. Gutro)

Our first hint that Ed was on vacation with us occurred as we were walking around the city's very crowded pedestrian shopping district. There on the ground, Tom spotted a 10 pence coin. As he reached down to pick it up, I said, "Ed's here." I immediately sensed that Ed was there, standing next to us, as the crowd bustled all around us.

What actually happened from Ed's perspective is that he was walking with us through the crowded street and suggested mentally to Tom that he should look down. Ed had already acted fast by apporting a coin from somewhere else to a spot just in front of Tom's path. Ed also suggested to Tom to look down, and that's when Tom found the coin.

I asked Tom if Ed ever went to England, and he replied, "No." Ed worked in landscaping and could never afford to travel overseas when he was alive. I told Tom, "Well, he's here with us now."

After touring the Roman Baths and the city of Bath, we returned to the rental car, with Ed's coin in Tom's pocket, and began the drive to Windsor. We would find out just how close Ed was to us.

###

Chapter 14
Amazing Rescue in England

This chapter originally appeared in my book "Ghosts of England on a Medium's Vacation."

Since Ed began talking with me in spirit, one of the things I've told him is that I wish I had met him in the physical world. Of course, I understand you can't turn back time, but I didn't think about how he could actually pull off something we were about to experience.

Spirits cross into the light and can travel anywhere at any time. They watch over us, wherever we go, and help us when needed. Fortunately, Ed's spirit was there when we needed him during our vacation in 2013.

Ed managed to appear to me in the form of a living, breathing man who looked as he would have looked, if he were alive today. What's more, Ed influenced his doppelganger to guide us out of a bad situation.

This adventure began when our rental car's global positioning system malfunctioned after working perfectly for several days. I thought it was odd how on the final leg of our trip that the GPS would suddenly malfunction and send us off-road. I later figured out that perhaps there was a reason.

GPS Unit Goes Haywire

When we picked up the rental car in London, we also rented a GPS unit for navigation purposes. Keep in mind that in 2013, MapQuest, Waze, and other driver navigation apps were not as prolific on cell phones as they are today. The only alternative to paper maps at that time was to rent a GPS unit.

We had planned out a route that began in London and extended out into the countryside to cities like Bath and Windsor.

As we departed Bath, we typed the address of our next destination into the GPS unit, which directed us to take the M6 motorway.

We had been driving for approximately one hour when the GPS unit directed us to take the next exit. Although we both thought the direction was odd, we thought the unit was diverting us to take a route that would avoid major traffic congestion closer to London.

Since the GPS unit had been accurate up until now, there was no reason to suspect that something was amiss. We took the exit and left the highway, soon finding ourselves driving on a two lane road. A short time later, the two lane road turned into a narrow country lane, with twists and turns. The GPS unit directed us to "go off road" and veer off the narrow lane onto a dirt road with grass growing in the center. We knew that something was not right. We backed out of the dirt road, and back onto the one lane road. We realized we were totally lost and likely would not able to figure out how to return to the highway. Anxiety was mounting because it was late and the sun had already dropped below the tree line.

We could not understand why the GPS unit had taken us so far off the road, and brought us to a dead-end.

Tom attempted to reprogram the GPS unit while I parked and got out of the car to search for a living person to ask for directions. However, it was a very rural area and the last house we had seen was at least a couple of miles behind us.

Houses in this area were spaced about a mile apart, and all had extremely long driveways. Finding a living person would take some doing.

The Arrival of Ed's Doppelganger

In the five minutes I was outside the car hoping someone would come along, a red Royal Mail truck came up over the hill behind us. I flagged down the driver and he pulled over. I couldn't believe our good fortune.

The driver stepped out of the truck; he was about my height, maybe a little taller, had a slender build, and a mop of black hair flecked with grey. His face was thin, and he wore glasses. I paused as I looked at him for a couple of seconds.

(Photo: Royal Mail Truck. Credit: FLICKR, Magners50)

I greeted the mailman and explained our predicament. I thought, "This guy looks really familiar to me." The mailman explained that after he made the three remaining deliveries on that road, he would show us the way back to the highway. I thanked him and returned to the car.

(Photo: Image of Ed around 1992.
Credit: Tom W.)

I got into the car and Tom said, "He looks just like I imagine Ed would look today." He continued, "If you recall the photos of Ed, just give him gray hair and glasses, and that's what our rescuer looks like."

I was astounded and I totally agreed. That's why he looked familiar. I had seen enough photographs of Ed to know that it very well could have been him, aged appropriately to be in his early 50s.

We followed Ed's doppelganger in the Royal Mail truck for several miles on what seemed to be an endless, winding road. Finally, that road connected back to the M6 motorway.

As the Royal Mail truck approached the exit to the highway, Ed's look-alike waved us off in the direction we needed to go. As he drove off in the opposite direction, I marveled at how spirits work. I truly feel as if I finally met Ed in person for the first time, after all these years.

The more I thought about that chance encounter with the Royal Mailman, the more clear it became that Ed had just responded to long held desire of mine: a wish to meet him in person.

Spirits Lead us to Doppelgangers

One common way that spirits let us know they are around us, is by leading us to someone who looks like them. Usually, the spirit will take us to someone they look like whom is either similar in age before they passed or a younger version of them.

This was the first time I've known of a spirit leading someone to a living person who looked like them had they continued to live and age.

Thinking About This Adventure

Because spirits and ghosts are energy, they have the ability to manipulate electronics, like a GPS unit. In hindsight, it's likely that Ed caused the GPS unit to malfunction. Of course, it took a lot of set up. He had to know that his look-alike would be driving a mail truck down that road soon after we stopped.

Obviously Ed can't come back in person, so he created the opportunity for me to meet someone that strongly resembled him.

Although it was Ed's greatest achievement from spirit, it wasn't his last one during our England trip. In the next chapter, you'll read how he used another sign from the past to remind us he was still on vacation with us.

###

Chapter 15
Sign of the M.O.T.

Earlier in this book, I discussed how spirits use unique signs to show us they are around. That's because common things usually don't have any personal meaning, so they really can't convey a spirit's presence. A message from spirit has to be something special, unique, or personal to someone who passed or to the person for whom the message is intended.

You may recall the story of how Ed influenced me to call Tom an "M.O.T."; an acronym for "mean old thing." Surprisingly, that acronym hadn't come up again for years.

After Ed's spirit rescue, he wanted to let us know that he was still with us while on our vacation. He wanted to assure us that his showing up "in person" wasn't just a one-time sign of his presence. So he went back in his "archive" of signs and pulled out an old one.

After our rescue and while on our drive to Windsor, Tom and I talked about Ed's doppelganger some more. We couldn't get over it. We were astounded that he actually found a man who very much resembled him, had he lived and aged, steered the man to find us in a remote location, and help us out. That's a lot of work for a spirit.

Once we arrived in London, the GPS unit was working fine and we managed to find the rental car return location. After we dropped the rental car off, we took a cab to our final destination on this trip - the Langdon House Bed and Breakfast in Windsor.

On the way, it became apparent that Ed was also in the cab with us. Although it was only for a split second, Tom glanced outside and saw a U.K. emissions testing sign that said "M.O.T. Testing." We later learned it means "Motor-vehicle Operations Testing. It was not a coincidence that he saw that acronym.

Actual Signs Can Be Signs!

Spirits can be pretty subtle in their communications. Sometimes the signs they give us can be actual physical signs with their name on it. Here's an example.

Let's say that your father's name was Matthew, and he passed away many years ago. You could be thinking of him as you perhaps drive by a church called "Saint Matthew's Church." That's not a coincidence. That's your dad's spirit letting you know that he's aware of your thoughts, and that he's sending you a clear message that he's still around.

Actual physical signs can be things like the name of a business or street names. Once you pay attention to these clues, you may be surprised how often spirit is guiding you.

During the summer of 2019, while on a vacation to Eastern Europe, I received a clear message from my mom. I was thinking of my parents as I was riding on a motor coach headed to Passau, Germany. At the border between Austria and Germany, there is now a gas station where there had once been a checkpoint. The large sign above the gas station read "Norma," my mother's name. It was clear to me that this was a sign from my mom letting me know that she was enjoying our trip with us.

We may miss coins, butterflies, or feathers, but when a spirit leads you to a sign with their name on it, they will likely be shaking their head if we miss it!

###

Chapter 16
A Push from my "Ghost Writer"

While working on this book in June, 2019, I sensed Ed was looking over my shoulder. One night in particular, I was tired, but felt like I needed to keep working.

That evening, I decided I would watch one television program and then work on the book. I thought, "I'll just make edits to one chapter," but wound up editing three of them, despite being tired.

I sensed that Ed was standing behind me as I sat typing at my computer desk. He kept saying to me, "Do more. Get this book finished." It felt like he was dictating what I should write, as I sit and type as he talks.

Ed kept pushing me to finish the book. He told me that he wants this book to be published before his birthday in October, so that initially was my goal.

He also told me that he's happy that he's been able to come through so much that he and I have developed a friendship that spans from life to afterlife.

His motivation in helping me write this book is for everyone. He said this book is important because it not only conveys many of the ways that all spirits try to communicate with their loved ones, but that spirits can maintain special relationships with the living from the other side.

###

Chapter 17
Rescued in the Street

In July 2019, Ed came to my rescue again and this time it was likely to avoid an accident.

When I took our four dogs for a walk in the neighborhood at 7:30 p.m., the sun was low in the summer sky. It had cooled off enough so that the asphalt pavement wouldn't burn their paws. The neighborhood has very few sidewalks; only the main streets have sidewalks on either side, while the side streets do not. So walking in the street is the only option. When I walk the dogs, I always stay close to the edge of the paved surface.

About 10 minutes into the walk, we were about to turn onto a familiar street, one that we have walked numerous times before. I suddenly felt a premonition that turning down that street was not a good idea. I tried to discount the feeling with my next thought, "That's the way I have to go to circle back to the house." I also wanted to walk the dogs for a longer period of time to tire them out before bedtime.

It was at this moment that I felt Ed's spirit grabbed my arm. I physically felt four cold fingers and a thumb grab my right bicep and squeeze it. I felt the pressure on my arm. Then I heard a male voice in my head say, "If you go that way, something bad will happen to one of the dogs." I immediately froze in my tracks.

It was Ed and he was giving me a stern warning. He was the one that put the premonition in my mind moments before he physical grabbed my arm. He realized that he had to give me a sterner "talking to" to avoid a bad event.

I looked down at the dogs, and two of them were looking right at me and at Ed's spirit, who was standing to my right side as he gripped my arm. It was all over in seconds.

I looked at the dogs and said, "No. We're not going that way. Turn around." They understand that command, so they all turned around and we headed back home. It was a very short walk, but I realized that Ed's warning likely saved one of us from being hit by a car.

As I entered the house with the dogs, I let out a big sigh of relief, "Thanks, Ed."

The lesson for everyone is that if you feel that you should or shouldn't do something or go somewhere, you're very likely being nudged by a spirit who is trying to take care of you. Listen to them. They only have your best interest at heart.

###

Chapter 18
Ed's Lessons to All

There are a number of lessons that you as the reader can take away from my amazing "supernatural" friendship with Ed.

Lesson #1: The Spirit Can be Anyone Remotely Connected

The first lesson is that spirits of loved ones, no matter how distantly related or how stretched the connection may be, even the friend of a friend, can come to us and let us know they are around. They can guide us out of a potentially bad situation by inspiring us to take a different direction while driving or walking, or perhaps even by suggesting that we departing at a later time. They can give us information for others whose grief may be blocking their ability to receive messages from their departed loved one. They can even come to our rescue, as Ed did on our trip to England.

What this all means is that is not necessary for you to have met that person in the physical plane for them to help you now that they are a spirit. Spirit connections supersede our finite earthly understanding of relationships, which are limited to friendships, family, or perhaps even someone that we may have met only once.

The spirits that are available to help you can be people like a great-great grandfather that you never met when he was alive in the physical realm. Perhaps your mother's third cousin or even a neighbor's relative who just passed may come into your dreams. The purpose of these kinds of dream messages from remote connections is often because the spirit can't get through the blocking grief that their loved may be experiencing. So if your neighbor's recently deceased husband comes to you in your dreams, he wants to get a message to his spouse that he is safe on the other side.

Lesson#2: Spirits Showing Up

The second lesson is that a particular spirit may keep coming to you. Perhaps they will toss coins in your path that are stamped with the year of their passing, week after week. That's because they feel a strong connection to you, and want to get to know you. Remember, when we pass and become a spirit (or choose to stay earthbound as a ghost) we maintain the same personalities that we had when we were living. So, yes, even spirits can want to befriend someone in the physical plane.

Lesson #3: Signs

The third lesson is that everyone should be vigilant for signs from spirit and not to easily dismiss them. Pay attention to dreams, coins and their dates, songs airing on the radio that remind you of someone just as you began thinking of them. Other indications that spirit is around you may be when you meet someone for the first time, and they have the same name as the person on the other side, or you may see someone that resembles someone you know that is now in spirit.

Spirits will also lead us to objects that will remind us of them or trigger a memory of them. Just as Ed told me to bring up an old silver car he once owned that inspired laughter among his friends.

Whatever the sign, the main message to you is that the spirit of your loved one continues to be around, even decades after they pass. The other side is timeless, just like the love we share for each other.

Lesson #4: What Spirits Want for Us

The fourth lesson here is that spirits want us to be happy. They don't want us to feel sad, guilty, or depressed. They want us to enjoy our lives and our time in the physical world.

Spirits also want us to know the truth about things that happened, especially when we don't have a true understanding. Just as Ed revealed that his passing was an accident.

Having us know the truth about certain things in their lives is something that's very important to spirit. In fact, that's why some people when the die, decide to stay earthbound as ghosts. Unfortunately, if they choose to become a ghost instead of crossing over, they're very limited in their abilities to go to different places, and cannot come into dreams.

Since dreams are likely the easiest and most effective way for someone who has passed to covey and image of something or show us a place where something precious to them may be located, that's all the more reason for someone not to stay behind and instead cross into the light and become a spirit.

Lesson #5: They're Waiting

The next lesson that Ed conveyed was that he, like the spirits of your loved ones, will be waiting for us in the light when it is our time to pass. Ed demonstrated that he was there in the light waiting to help my dog, Sprite, cross over in July 2013. He also acknowledged that my dog, Buzz, who passed in 2005, had found him and was there with him also.

Just as Ed, my dad, and Buzz's spirit showed up at the veterinarian's office at Sprite's time, your relatives, friends, and/or pets will also be there for you. Often when people are close to their time of transition, they report seeing relatives in spirit present in the room.

Not only do they come to guide us into the light, but they know that the transition to the afterlife is unsettling and can be even frightening. So they come to help us cross over and give us the love and reassurance that crossing over is the right thing to do, and that everything will be okay.

Lesson #6: They are Alive in the Light

The sixth lesson Ed taught me is that spirits of our loved ones, whether person or animal, are still very much alive in the afterlife.

We can't think of them as physical beings, because they are beings of energy now. They do maintain the memories, personalities and knowledge that they had here in their physical lives. However, they don't have a job or a career in the afterlife like we have on Earth. They are part of a greater, boundless love energy (some call it god-energy) that has the ability to travel anywhere, anytime and can be in different places at the same time.

Spirits do come into our dreams to let us know they are perfectly fine in the afterlife. Usually, a spirit will appear in a peaceful dream setting, like a grassy field, park, or beach. You may dream of them at a party or sitting in your home. They convey these images because that's what we associate with comfort in the physical world.

If you want a spirit to come into your dreams ask them each night before you go to bed. Eventually, they will be able to do so.

Lesson #7: Timing of Messages

As Ed showed over and over, birthdays, anniversaries and holidays were the prime times for his reappearances. The same goes for spirits of your loved ones, too. That's because those are usually the times we reach out to our living loved ones. We wish someone a happy birthday or anniversary or holiday. Spirits acknowledge those dates from the other side.

That's not to say that a spirit won't come through to you on any day or date. They will. Just as Ed came through and sent us a Royal Mail truck to save us in England on May. May is not associated with any birthday, anniversary or holiday that has a relation to us or Ed.

Those special times are just the most common times for spirts to communicate. Those are certainly not the only times they may come around.

The Final Rule

The biggest thing to remember is that when it comes to spirits, there is no such thing as a coincidence.

Final Words

I hope that you've enjoyed reading this amazing story of a man I never knew in the physical world, and managed to befriend him as a spirit.

One thing I do that you may find helpful is to think of your loved ones who have passed as just living in another state or living in another part of the country. That's because the certainly do show up from time to time.

The best part about having relatives, friends and pets in spirit is that they will show up from time to time to steer us clear of trouble and keep us safe. They can also hear you anytime, anywhere and anyplace you go. There's just no calling, emailing or texting required to reach them, only love.

###

Bibliography

Chan, Sewell and James Barron (contributing) (6 February 2008). "City Room: Heath Ledger's Death Is Ruled an Accident." The New York Times. Retrieved 17 August 2008.

About the Author

(Photo: Rob with Dolly, Franklin and Tyler. Credit: Tom W.)

Rob considers himself an average guy, who just happens to be able to hear, feel, sense and communicate with earthbound ghosts and spirits.

When not communicating with the dead, Rob communicates with the living. He's a meteorologist by trade who enjoys talking about weather. Rob worked as a radio broadcast meteorologist at the Weather Channel. He has almost 20 years of on-air radio broadcasting experience.

Rob enjoys taking ghost walks in various cities and visiting historic houses and sites to see who is still lingering behind and encourages them to move into the light to find peace.

Rob is an avid dog lover who, with his husband, volunteers with Dachshund and Weimaraner dog rescues. Together, they've fostered and transported many dogs, assessing the dogs at shelters for the rescues, working with coordinators, vets, and shelters to save the lives of dogs.

He still reads and collects comic books and has always loved the mysterious heroes. Since he was a boy, one of his favorite superheroes has always been the ghostly avenger created in the 1940s called "The Spectre."

If you would be interested in having Rob speak about how our pets provide messages from the other side, or about ghosts and spirits, please contact him through email or his blog. To share stories or questions write Rob at Rgutro@gmail.com

Website: www.robgutro.com or www.petspirits.com
Blog: http://ghostsandspiritsinsights.blogspot.com/
Facebook pages:
https://www.facebook.com/RobGutroAuthorMedium
https://www.facebook.com/ghostsandspirits.insightsfromamedium
Twitter: https://twitter.com/GhostMediumBook
Amazon Author Page: http://amazon.com/author/robgutro
YouTube: https://plus.google.com/collection/ok7wh

Other Books by Rob Gutro: "Pets and the Afterlife; Pets and the Afterlife 2; Lessons Learned from Talking to the Dead; Ghosts and Spirits, Ghosts of England on a Medium's Vacation.
Available in paperback and E-book, on Amazon.com

Made in the USA
Middletown, DE
27 July 2019